LIONS

A PORTRAIT OF THE ANIMAL WORLD

LEE SERVER

TODTRI

This book was designed and produced by TODTRI Book Publishers
P.O. Box 572, New York, NY 10116-0572 FAX: (212) 695-6984

e-mail : info@todtri.com

Printed and bound in Korea

ISBN 1-57717-079-2

Visit us on the web!
www.todtri.com

Author: Lee Server

Publisher: Robert M. Tod
Editor: Edward Douglas
Assistant Editor: Elaine Luthy
Book Designer: Mark Weinberg
Typesetting: Command-O Design

PHOTO CREDITS
Photo Source/Page Number

INTRODUCTION

The pride is the core of the lion's family life. Based on blood relationship through the female line, a close-knit, organized group of lions cooperates in hunting prey, defending territory, and raising young.

T*he majestic lion is the legendary ruler of the animal kingdom. Revered for its strength and bravery, the lion has been a symbol of supremacy since the beginning of recorded history.*

The lion gained its ascendancy in a world filled with fierce contenders. It is not the largest of animals, nor the strongest or fastest. Compared to other cats, its skills as a hunter are, in fact, flawed, and its plain, tawny coat does not compare to the richly colored and patterned fur of other animals of its kind.

Still, to humans, its position remains uncontested. Certainly, there are few people who, having seen a full-grown lion in the wild, would question its superiority. This has much to do with bearing. The lion conveys grandeur and self-assurance, particularly a mature adult male possessing a magnificent, full mane that appears to confer the same rank and authority as a king's ceremonial headdress.

Then there is the undoubted fierceness of the lion in battle as it attacks and destroys its prey. Its victory is followed by a triumphant roar: a low grumble building in intensity and proclaiming territoriality and power throughout the lion's domain. Equally impressive is the typically catlike aura of intelligence that conveys the sense of a subtly scheming mind at work. For such things and more is the lion justly awarded its crown.

Because of these attributes, observed by people through the ages, this splendid cat has long represented both human and supernatural power. The lion's body was used to depict the Egyptian sphinx, which in various representations has the head of a ram, hawk, or human. Usually standing for courage and domination, the lion is a symbolic motif in the Bible and also appears in many folktales, including Aesop's fables.

The lion's designation as the King of Beasts can be traced back to writings from the first century of the Christian era. Lions frequently figured in the heraldic devices and coats-of-arms of medieval nobility and were elements in the royal family crests of such kingdoms as England, Scotland, Denmark, Norway, and Belgium. Richard I, the twelfth-century English king and veteran of the Crusades to the Holy Land was hailed throughout Europe as Richard Coeur de Lion, or Richard the Lion-Hearted, for his bravery in battle. In various parts of Asia, the lion was frequently depicted as a symbol of power and strength—even in China, to which it is not indigenous.

Down through the ages the raw and savage power of lions has been exploited in the presentation of such spectacles as the wild animal fights in the Roman arena, where their ferocity was unleashed on unarmed men and women for the delight of cheering crowds. In recent times and up to the present, these big cats and others have added a sense of danger to the performances of lion tamers, who are star attractions in circuses around the world.

Not content with vicarious thrills, the big game hunters of the recent past sought an almost visceral excitement in confronting such a fierce beast as the lion and becoming its victor. For almost a century, lion hunting on safari conferred status and prestige to those who could afford it, and in an almost magical way, endowed the conquering, gun-bearing hunter with the very attributes of strength and courage that the lion was believed to possess.

Yet, for all the inferred symbolism and self-projection by humans, the reality of the lion's life and behavior is even more intriguing than the mythology it has inspired. Observation and study of this animal reveals its place in the natural order and encourages closer examination of the intricate web of life to which we belong.

Lionesses can be caring mothers, guarding their cubs in infancy, entertaining them with play, and finally, teaching them to hunt and provide for themselves.

As he yawns in the afternoon sun, this male lion, with his thick-maned head and fearsome teeth, shows clearly why he is regarded as the King of Beasts.

THE NATURE OF LIONS

Lions are members of the cat family, whose original ancestors have been traced back some twelve million years. The various types of cats have actually changed very little in all that time.

The proper family name for cats is Felidae. Under this heading are four genera, or groupings of cats: *Felis*, *Neofelis*, *Panthera*, and *Acinonyx*. Both the *Acinonyx* and *Neofelis* groups contain a single species each: the cheetah and the clouded leopard respectively. The genus *Felis* includes all the smaller cats from the fierce American puma, or mountain lion, to the common domestic house cat. The remaining cats all belong to the genus *Panthera*. These include the big cats of legend, the roaring royalty of jungle, forest, and savanna: leopards, snow leopards, jaguars, tigers, and, of course, lions.

Despite their very different worlds and ways of living, the various groups of cats remain close cousins in a variety of ways. Unlikely as it may seem, the untamed African lion has much in common with the pampered pussycat curled up in an armchair. People observing lions in the wild are often struck by how frequently the huge and dangerous animals assume the poses and display the personality traits of a pet tabby. Similarly, the house cat, domesticated a mere five thousand years ago—a fraction of the time (50,000 years) that the dog has been tamed—has retained hunting instincts and feral abilities that link it to the regal lion. As for the lion, natural scientists are only now just beginning to understand the capacity for diversity and adaptation of it is capable.

In repose, this mature male lion projects the inscrutable nature and sense of authority that have made it a legendary symbol for people throughout history.

From Prehistory to the Present

It was only in recent times that lions became known as exclusively African animals. As far back as ten thousand years ago, they could be found widely distributed, not only in most of Africa, but throughout large portions of Europe, Asia, North America, and northern South America. The earliest human records of lions are preserved on the walls of caves in southwestern France dating to the latter part of the last ice age. There, etched into the rock, are silhouettes of a European subspecies known to modern science as the cave lion.

Gradually, as the character of European forests changed, lions abandoned the region, and by the time of the Greek Golden Age they could only be found in Europe in the Balkan Peninsula. They were reportedly common in Greece around 500 B.C., but by 300 B.C. Aristotle had described them as rare. Four hundred years later, in A.D.100, it was recorded that lions had not been seen in the region for some time. However, they continued to exist in Palestine for many more centuries, finally disappearing from that area around the time of the Crusades.

The shrinking of the lion's range is directly related to the kind of habitat it needs to survive. Despite being known as the King of the Jungle, the lion actually prefers areas of sparse

Every part of the lion's body contributes to its effectiveness as a predator. Its jaws, teeth, shoulders, and legs can exert overwhelming force, while the large paws are powerful enough to stun and bring down prey.

Following page: The lion's strong legs enable it to leap and attack either prey or enemies. This ability is also useful in entering trees, which lions do for a variety of reasons. Though not as agile and skilled as leopards, they are nonetheless quite competent climbers.

tree growth. Most lions live in grassy plains, savannas, open woodlands, and among thorny scrub trees. Historically, as their habitats have lost these characteristics, either through natural change or human intervention, the lion has departed or been driven out.

The lion's departure from Europe in prehistoric times was most likely the result of the massive spreading of forests throughout the continent, making the area uninhabitable for these cats. In other parts of the world, the growth of human settlements and agriculture changed the nature of wild plains and grasslands, gradually driving the lion from its ranges in India, the Middle East, and northern Africa. Today, except for a small population of animals in India's Gir Forest, the once vast range of the lion has been reduced to Central Africa, chiefly in the game parks and reserves of Kenya and Tanzania.

Built to Kill

Among the big cats, the lion is second only to the tiger in size. The average male lion's weight ranges from 350 to 400 pounds (157 to 180 kilograms), though some individuals may

Vultures are quick to find a lion's kill and move in to steal as much of it as they can. Here, a young lion leaps through the air to disperse the flock of thieves.

be as heavy as 500 pounds (225 kilograms). Females are smaller and can weigh considerably less than males. The normal length of the male is 9 feet (2.7 meters), while the female is usually about 8 feet (2.4 meters) long.

The lion's body completely suits the needs of a predator. When hunting, the great strength of its shoulder and forelegs is employed with full force, as it quickly runs from cover and leaps through the air to secure a stranglehold on the neck of a large animal. At this point, the large, powerful jaws come into play to

Once a creature has been killed, the lion may drag the carcass to a safe, secluded spot where it can feed without the interruptions of scavengers or other predators.

Lions are swift and efficient killers. They either strangle their victims by an attack on the throat or suffocate them by covering the mouth and nostrils.

A young elephant is soon dispatched by the lion's powerful bite into its neck. The sheer weight and strength of the lion is enough to overcome this animal, even though it is larger than the cat.

Though lions are not as well known for leaping as many other members of the cat family, they are still capable of springing great distances and great heights. The maximum leap of a lion has been measured at 40 feet (12.1 meters). This jumping ability also enables them to enter trees. Other cats are quicker, more skillful climbers, but lions can still reach quite lofty perches. They tend to climb more when they are young and agile, and older, heavier lions may not be able to climb at all.

A lion's mouth is equipped with thirty teeth that are large and impressive and of more use in gripping and subduing prey than in consuming it. The four largest teeth are the razor sharp canines, which are effective killing tools. Then, there are four carnassial teeth, capable of cutting through skin and other tough material such as tendons between muscles and bones. The tongue, which is exceptionally coarse, aids in rasping apart meat and preparing it for digestion. But since its teeth are not designed for chewing food finely, the lion must swallow its meal in chunks.

either choke or suffocate the victim. If a smaller creature is attacked, the paws are used to knock down and kill the prey. These paws are particularly large and conceal long claws that are used to hook into and hold struggling animals. Since they are retractable and are extended only when needed, the claws are able to maintain their sharpness. Once prey has been killed, the lion uses its claws while feeding to remove excessively large chunks of meat from its teeth.

Though capable of short bursts of speed of up to 30 miles (48 kilometers) per hour, the lion is not always successful in catching its intended victim. Some animals bolt and dash quickly out of reach. The lion's lack of stamina makes it incapable of long, hard pursuits.

The lion's differently shaped teeth are variously designed for holding, killing, and cutting. Since these teeth are of little help in chewing, the lion must swallow its food in large chunks.

The lion's coat is well designed for stealth. Blending in with the grasses in which it stalks its prey, the lion is able to use the element of surprise in subduing unsuspecting creatures.

Walking with its head slightly lowered and its gaze fixed forward, this lioness is undoubtedly menacing. The amber glow of her typically feline eyes suggests cold calculation and the potential for swift, deadly attack.

Distinguishing Features

The coloration of the lion's coat, whether male or female, is widely varied. It ranges from light tan and silvery gray to yellowish red and dark reddish brown. Each of these hues allows the cat to conceal itself in tall grasses and other vegetation when awaiting or stalking prey. The animal's underbelly is lighter in color, almost pale cream, while the ears and the tip of the tail are covered with black fur.

Of all the cats, only male lions have manes. There are both heavy- and light-maned males, displaying many different shadings of color. For most males, all parts of the head, except the face, are covered with thick, heavy hair that extends down to the neck and shoulders. This dense covering, which provides protection during fights, begins to form on the heads of young males soon after the first year of life and reaches it full growth when the males are five years old. Mane coloration is usually a mixture of black, brown, and yellow, with one of the three colors predominant. As the lions age, the manes darken.

Among the lion's other distinguishing features are its amber eyes. They are considerably wider than the human eye, measuring more than 1.5 inches (37 millimeters) in diameter, compared to man's 0.9-inch (23-millimeter) eye. As with all cats, the lion's eyes are set fairly close together at the front of the head, providing good forward binocular vision that enables the lion to judge distances accurately during a hunt. Both day and night vision are excellent.

The prominent mane of the male lion is a unique feature. It serves to make the large head even more intimidating, and offers protection from injury during combat.

An even more distinctive feature, and one that sets the lion apart from all other species, is its roar. Under certain weather conditions, the roar can be heard at distances of more than 5 miles (8 kilometers), and is created by the lion as it stands, bends its head down slightly, and greatly expands its chest to produce a sound of such power that often great dust clouds are stirred up.

This display is made soon after sundown, after a kill, and after eating. It is believed to be an expression of territorial right and, perhaps, of contentment.

Lions produce at least eight other vocalizations which include low grunts to maintain contact with other individuals, growls to signify anger, and the soft calling sounds used by mothers to control their cubs.

After a long, sound sleep, the lion slowly resumes its activities. With a few wide yawns and long, sinuous stretches, the big cat prepare its body for the exertions of the hunt.

A snarling male lion advances forward to repel an intruder. The lion's fearsome size and strength, combined with its fierce growls and roars, make it an able defender of its territory.

LION COMMUNITIES

Lions, more than any other members of the cat family, are social animals. Most of them live in groups known as prides, which usually number ten to twenty individuals but can include as many as thirty-five. Prides are composed of related females, their cubs, and perhaps as many as five nonpermanent males, who are associated with the group for about three years. The lionesses, that make up the core of the pride, almost always live together for their entire lives.

Male cubs are generally expelled from the pride after two years, while their female siblings remain as permanent members of the group. Males driven from a pride usually band together and roam from place to place, until they reach the age of five years. At this age they are fully mature, and are ready to find a new pride, drive off the incumbent males, and assume leadership of the core of females and their kin.

Once established, the new male group—numbering two to five—works vigilantly to keep intruders, particularly other males, from disrupting the social structure. They also do not allow nonpride members to hunt in their territory. Interlopers are warned to stay away from the area by the roaring of the males, and

A few members of a typical pride find rest on the plains of Kenya's Masai Mara Game Reserve. Here are seen five adult females and two of the pride's dominant, protecting males.

Preparing the next generation for life is the most basic function of the pride, a social structure unique to lions within the cat family. The close knit female members of the pride share equally in the care and raising of the young.

by the liquid scent they leave on bushes and trees to mark the boundaries of their territory. Any stranger that persists and refuses to leave must be ready for a violent fight. The male lions also end disturbances that take place within the pride itself.

While the males concern themselves with these arduous tasks, the females take on most of the responsibility of hunting prey. Studies have shown that the male lion kills only 12 percent of its own food, while the female supplies it with 75 percent. The remaining 13 percent represents the kills of other predators, which the male lion simply takes as his own. When the females hunt, they leave their young alone for a considerable time, sometimes as much as forty-eight hours. Because of this, many of the unprotected cubs left behind are often killed by hyenas, leopards, and even other lions.

Territory and Family Life

Because of their social nature, individual pride members do not claim their own separate territories, but instead, the pride as a whole shares a common hunting area. Because the total area of habitats suited to lions has become much smaller over the years, some pride territories overlap. There is always the potential for serious conflicts among the different groups, but in general, they are able to inhabit the same region peacefully.

The amount of available food and water determines how much space each pride requires. If there is abundant prey, the group usually covers an area of up to 15 square miles (39 square kilometers). However, if food is more difficult to obtain, the pride's territory may have to be expanded to as much as 100 square miles (260 square kilometers).

The weather is a determining factor in food availability. For instance, during the rainy season lions in woodland areas find the movements and numbers of their prey erratic and undependable. This is not such a problem for lions on the plains, where prey animal populations remain relatively stable. However, during wet periods, woodland lions must expand their range considerably in order to sustain themselves. But with the return of dry

Two lionesses escort a group of five cubs, ready to protect them from any threat. All adult female members of a pride cooperate in caring for and looking after the young.

A male lion chases a rival male away from the pride he dominates. Males must constantly be on guard against threats from other males, eager to take over a group of females and assert their own rule.

weather, the herds, upon which all lions depend, become more reliable in their behavior, allowing lions in all habitats to cover a smaller area in the search for food.

Lion family life is, for the most part, relatively serene, at least by the standards of the wild. Of course, lions within a pride fight on occasion, and in rare instances one pride member may kill another. However, such an occurrence is exceptional, and not at all typical of the average lion family. The pride is structured and disciplined, with ranking members—protecting males and dominant females—leading subordinates and cubs. Each individual has its role, and as a rule, orderly procedures are followed.

However, when food is available lions are at their most asocial. It is at feeding time that fights are most likely to occur. The reason for this is that food is taken according to

Following page: Having eaten their fill, these two females leave the carcass to the cubs, while they warily guard against intruders.

Aside from his genetic contribution, the male lion uses his strength and fierce demeanor to protect the pride, shielding it and its territories from the incursions of other lions and rival predators.

Lionesses drinking at a water hole are always on the alert. As they arrive to drink, most other animals will leave. However, lionesses, especially in small numbers, run the risk of attack from large packs of hyenas.

the rank and strength of each member, with the strongest claiming the largest and choicest portions. Rivalry, defense of rank, and sheer hunger combine to produce a meal marked by hissing, snapping, and growling as the pride squabbles over division of the carcass. However, after feeding, the lions return to the normal tranquillity of their lives. Even members recently in conflict over food often show affection toward one another.

Lions may sleep or rest for as much as twenty hours a day. When active and not in pursuit of food, they sometimes roam about, often covering a range of 5 miles (8 kilometers) in a single day. However, when hunting, they may, if need be, travel as much as 15 miles (24 kilometers).

This male lion, in a state of complete relaxation, has seemingly been transformed from a fierce predator to the most beguiling and harmless of animals, the house cat.

With his paw over his eyes, a male lion sleeps soundly. Like other cats, lions require a good deal of rest and can sleep up to twenty hours a day.

Establishing Bonds

Members of a pride may separate from time to time, with individuals wandering in various directions to amble about their territory. When the group comes together again, the lions exchange friendly greetings by rubbing cheeks, shaking heads, and grunting. Pride members have a common scent, which is borne by liquid secreted from the skin just above the eye. This enables the lions to recognize one another and to detect any intruder into the group.

Often, when lions meet they groom each other affectionately by licking their neighbor's head and neck. Their rough, strong tongues are ideally suited for cleaning and combing fur. This is particularly needed after a meal, when their coats are often covered with blood. Dirt, ticks, and other parasites are also removed in this manner.

Mutual grooming is an activity shared largely by females and larger cubs. Adult males are rarely involved in this social activity, most likely due to the difficulty in cleaning the heavy hair of the male's mane. As for

A major grooming problem for the male lion is the care of his massive, furry mane. Though he also has difficulty cleaning his face properly, the rest of his body is kept very clean.

self-grooming, lions keep their bodies quite clean, but due their difficulty in maintaining a posture that frees the front paws, they are unable to keep their faces in the same condition.

Play is another means of bonding among pride members. Females play frequently, while adult males are less enthusiastic. Lionesses teasingly stalk and wrestle with other females, and also romp a great deal with cubs.

The rituals of meeting and mutual grooming provide an important bond between the members of a pride that helps to maintain the group's cohesion and structure. Though most lions enjoy these lifelong social relationships, a certain percentage are unattached nomads.

When pride members meet after being apart for awhile, they greet each other by rubbing heads to show their friendly intentions. The greeting is often followed by a period of mutual grooming.

Lion cubs that survive the dangers and rigors of the first year of life remain close to their mother and learn her hunting skills. They remain with her for some time, often for more than two years.

While male lions avoid such frivolous activity, females enjoy bouts of play, especially with the young. This is not only bonding behavior but is also a means of developing alertness and bodily coordination in the growing cubs.

Frequently, a mother playfully pokes a youngster with her paw, causing the cub to swat back, often while rolling on its back. Since they have not yet achieved sufficient coordination, the youngest cubs cannot enjoy the sport of running and stalking but are content to roll around and grapple one another.

While older lions play in pairs, young cubs are able to amuse themselves without companions. They often find sticks to carry and throw about, sometimes leading to competitions with their littermates who try to capture the object themselves. Cubs are also known to delight in attacking and biting the tufted tail of an adult male, usually resulting in a growling, roaring reprimand.

The cooperative nature of the pride is shown by the treatment healthy members bestow on old, sick, or injured comrades. Those who are fit hunt food for the few who are unable to do so. However, when lions are old and very weak, they themselves become prey to other carnivores, usually hyenas or wild dogs. As a result, lions in the wild do not survive to die peacefully of old age.

Nomadic Lions

In contrast to lions that live in the ordered social structure of the pride, there are others that choose a different way of life. These are the nomadic, or migratory, lions. Some young males, when expelled from the pride of their birth, do not seek to join and rule other prides. Instead, they spend their lives wandering. Often, they are joined by other wandering males, as well as females, who in various ways have been separated from their close female relatives. Females make up about a third of the total number of nomadic lions.

Thorough research of these animals has revealed that only about 10 percent of the nomads remain solitary. Ninety percent become associated with a series of temporary groups that are much less rigid and less organized than conventional prides. Most of these casual nomadic groups are small, with no more than two to four members at any given time. However, some may include a dozen or more animals.

Aside from the usually small number of members in these groups, there are several

A small lion cub provokes the King of the Jungle with a playful nip. As a rule, male lions are tolerant of these youthful pranks and are content to snarl and growl until the nuisance goes away.

A sleepy cub harmlessly bites the neck of a sibling. Like all youngsters, cubs are curious and energetic and will persist in their playful antics until they drop from exhaustion.

Lion cubs spend a great deal of time grappling and swatting one another. These playful sparring matches teach basic defensive skills and help to establish patterns of dominance and rank among the younger generation.

Three lionesses rest beneath a tree, saving their energy for the nighttime hunt. Areas as open as this one provide little concealing cover, so stalking prey is more successful in total darkness.

other distinctions between nomadic lions and pride lions. First of all, there is no genetic relationship between members of nomadic groups, as there is in prides. Secondly, while pride lions generally remain in their group for life and drive away most intruders, nomadic groups are not nearly as restrictive. Members arrive and depart frequently, and new associations are formed without conflict. Many contacts made between nomads last only a few hours, while others may continue for several days. Nomads frequently wander in and out of several groups during a short period, and may encounter a half dozen or more lions within the span of a few days. With so many different contacts,

each nomad soon begins to come across previous acquaintances, making it easier to from casual groups.

Nomads tend to be open and accepting toward each other, because they are not deeply territorial. Some nomadic groups do defend certain land areas on occasion, but these are exceptional. Without the pride lions' disciplined, lifelong association with close family members and their common interest in protecting traditional hunting grounds, the nomads are free agents, tied to no group and to no particular territory. They are, therefore, less wary and less hostile to strangers and are able to shift easily from group to group as they continue their wanderings.

The width of this tree branch, with its forked extensions, seems perfectly designed for a sleeping lion. The elevated perch provides not only shade but the possibility of a gentle breeze and escape from biting flies that hover over the ground below.

MOTHERS AND CUBS

The act of mating is fast and frequent, occurring many times over several days, and often accompanied by growling and snapping.

Though lions are capable of breeding throughout the year, some seasonal patterns have been observed. In the wilds of the Serengeti, as well as in South Africa's Kruger National Park, most breeding takes place from March to June. However, in western Africa, as well as in India, the lions tend to mate from October to December. If a female does not become pregnant during these periods, another breeding cycle usually occurs within three months.

During mating periods, males and females are together constantly, with the females in heat from four to eight days. Lions may copulate as many as forty times a day, and in some instances, even higher numbers have been

If she decides her den is no longer safe, the mother lion finds a new one and transports her cubs to it, one by one, in her mouth.

counted. The actual mating only lasts about six seconds, and often concludes with the male lightly biting the female's neck. To this, she usually responds with a swing of a paw and a low growl.

The Role of Genetics

The permanent members of any given pride are all closely related females. The group is composed of mothers, daughters, granddaughters, sisters, aunts, nieces, and cousins. Young males born into a pride are not permanent members but are driven away a year or two after birth to fend for themselves. Usually, the outcasts stay together, and upon reaching adulthood, may eventually become companions in dominating and mating with a new group of females.

These new ruling males—generally two to five in number—might possibly be brothers, but since their mother may have mated with more than one male, they may not have had the same father, even though they are littermates. In fact, if they came from a sizable birth pride with a significant number of dominant males, they may be only distantly related.

Thus, the social organization and behavior of lions protects against inbreeding. Even though the all-female prides are close relatives—albeit with different fathers—their mates, springing from altogether separate prides, provide a broad genetic heritage.

In addition, the pattern of dominant males being periodically displaced by younger, stronger ones ensures that succeeding generations will flourish. The genes of the conquering males are passed on to their offspring, along with the strong hunting capabilities and instincts of the prospering lionesses. Through the process of natural selection, the traits of the able males and females are continued, enabling lions to produce high-quality replicas of themselves.

Following page: Having attained a perch in a low tree, this cub is mischievously preparing to pounce on one of his playmates from above.

Courtship and mating can be dangerous for lions. The large male will tolerate no intruders, and the female will not mate until she is ready.

Though the mating of two lions is often a violent affair, it nonetheless ends peacefully with both partners contented.

As mating concludes, the male appears to reaffirm the bond by giving his partner an almost affectionate bite on the back of her neck.

Lionesses bear their young in sheltered dens where they care for them for the first six weeks of their lives. When they are strong enough, she leads them out to join her pride.

Lionesses rarely have litters of more than four cubs. This number is the most that they can suckle at a time. Because of this feeding problem, it is unlikely that all members of a larger litter would survive infancy.

Birth

The gestation period of the female lion is between 105 and 115 days. Before giving birth, the female seeks a site that provides protection from cold, wind, excessive sunlight, and moisture. In the dry season, most lionesses find a sheltered place near rivers or reeds. In the rainy season, the pregnant lioness prefers higher ground amid rocks or safe spots in hills. Not only must the refuge provide protection from the elements and access to water, but it must also camouflage her cubs from enemies that might prey on them while she is foraging for food. There may even be occasions when the mother changes the location of her family to ensure greater safety. When she does, she moves the cubs one at a time, carrying them in her mouth.

Most lionesses bear litters of two to four cubs, although in captivity some have had as many as nine. In the wild it is unlikely that more than four cubs could survive. Since the mother has only four nipples, more than four cubs could not obtain sufficient nourishment, and the stronger ones would soon outdistance the weaker siblings.

At birth, each cub is about 1 foot (30.5 centimeters) long and weighs close to 1 pound (0.45 kilogram). Lion cubs are born covered with fur that is spotted with gray patches of varying shapes; their wide tails are untufted. The eyes are closed and do not open for two weeks or more. After three weeks, the milk teeth begin to appear, and within another week, the cubs are able to take their first bites of meat, though they will continue to suckle for at least six months.

Raising the Young

In any given pride, the successfully mated lionesses tend to give birth at about the same time. Each individual female seeks sheltered solitude to bear her young. Having done so, the mother lions stay away from the other members of the pride for about six weeks before rejoining the group with their cubs in

A cub playfully attacks the hindquarter of a retreating female. The youngster's red paw indicates that a meal has just been completed.

Though plants are not a part of his diet, this young lion wants to try the taste of one. He also seems to find that the twig makes a useful tool for removing food from between the teeth.

These cubs may be just learning that, since they are lions, climbing is not their greatest skill. One day they will be able to climb, but in the meantime, this practice strengthens muscles and sharpens claws.

tow. When the young are old enough to move about on their own, several mothers often form a group. The cubs in this group nurse not only from their mother but from any available lactating female. The responsibility of caring for the cubs is shared by all the mothers, who protect each one as if it were their own. It is also not unusual for a female of the pride without cubs to shield and watch over the youngsters.

Male lions take little part in raising cubs, except as defenders of the pride as a whole. In general, they are tolerant of the young, even when they try to take food from the adults' mouths or playfully bite their tails. However, these are dangerous games, for a sufficiently irritated male can cause great injury or even death to an overly exuberant cub. Fortunately, this is a rare occurrence, and for the most part, youthful antics are gently rebuffed.

Cubs can be less fortunate if rival males suddenly appear, drive away the defending males, and take over the pride. The new conquerors will then kill most of the small cubs, thus stimulating the females of the pride to breed. The resulting offspring will, of course, be those of the new males, and these will have a better

Cubs are defenseless during their first months of life. Since mothers must leave them unguarded to hunt for food, they are protected only by their spotted fur, which provides a concealing camouflage as they lie hidden in dense vegetation.

chance of survival without other, larger cubs competing with them for food.

Growing Up

Young lions begin to follow their mothers in the quest for food around the age of three months. However, they do not take an active part in hunting forays until they are weaned about three months later. Before that, their role is generally limited to watching and stumbling along behind.

A most dangerous time for the growing young lions occurs between their ninth and

A lioness relaxes in the sun as she suckles her three cubs. The male lion plays little part in raising the young, and may be driven away by the female if he tries to approach them.

In a moment of tenderness, two cubs find comfort beside a male lion. Adult males are rarely close to the young and tolerate them at best, but this drowsy lion is not bothered by their equally sleepy presence.

Learning the social rituals of meeting and grooming is an important part of a cub's education. The bonds forged in infancy last a lifetime for many lions.

twelfth months. This is when the permanent teeth begin appear, bringing with them a great deal of pain, the possibility of infection and fever, and a dangerous level of restlessness. For these reasons, there is a high mortality rate during this period of development.

Most of the lions that survive the dangers and rigors of their first year of life continue to hunt with their mothers for quite some time. Mother and cubs remain together for one and a half to two years. After this time the lioness mates again and prepares to raise a new litter, leaving the older offspring to fend for themselves. The young females, though no longer protected by their mother, remain in the pride and band together for a while, until they reach sexual maturity. The young males either leave the pride of their own accord or are driven from it to begin the adult portion of their lives.

Lion cubs that survive the perils of infancy hunt with their mothers for some time, often for as long as two years. This apprenticeship makes them thoroughly capable of providing for themselves in adulthood.

LIONS AS HUNTERS

The kinds of animals suitable as prey for such a carnivore as the lion vary with the habitats in which the big cats live. The scrub and grassland areas, in which most lions live, are filled with many grazing herd animals. These herbivorous creatures—wildebeests, zebras, antelopes, gazelles, and waterbucks—are the lion's primary sources of food. Lions also have a fondness for warthogs and have been known to wait many hours for them to emerge from the safety of their burrows in the ground.

However, if a lion is hungry enough and unable to find the food it prefers, it will eat anything it can catch, including fish. Lions will also go after such large animals as water buffalo and giraffes, even though an attack against these stronger creatures is difficult. Many lions have been injured trying to take the larger animals, and some have been so severely crippled that they were unable to provide for themselves again.

Stalking By Night

Lions hunt mostly under cover of darkness, when it is easier to move within striking distance of unsuspecting animals. It is common

Lions must be patient animals, since most of their hunts fail. A noted study determined that out of sixty-one observed attacks, only ten were successful.

for lions to watch their prey during daylight, usually just before sunset, and then wait patiently until dark before making the kill. Similarly, if there is bright moonlight, they will sit quietly until the moon is obscured, and then move forward to take their victim.

Hunting during the day is highly inefficient due to the lack of adequate cover in such habitats as the savannas and plains. Quite often, when a lion moves toward an animal in full light, the prey will quickly spot its foe and make an escape. However, lions living in areas of denser vegetation are more successful daytime hunters.

Though nocturnal hunting is the best strategy in open country, there are some occasions when the brightness of the sun provides tempting opportunities. At the height of

To obtain such a favored food animal as the warthog, pride teamwork is used to surround the creature's burrow and wait patiently in place. When the animal begins to emerge, the group pounces forward to dig it completely out of the ground and subdue it.

The lion's strong jaws clamp tightly on the head of a wildebeest, quickly suffocating it. Later the prey will be ripped open by powerful canine teeth.

almost total darkness. As a lion slowly stalks its prey—freezing one moment, then creeping forward the next—the eyes are constantly fixed on the path and behavior of the victim. In areas where tall grasses grow, the lion takes advantage of the cover to conceal its stealthy movements. However, as the cat advances, it checks the nearness of its goal by raising its head up and out of the hiding place to gauge the distance. In doing so, the lion may give itself away and startle the prey into flight. But if it doesn't, the final pursuit begins, with the ensuing charge and attack coordinated completely by the eye.

Acute hearing is also effective in detecting prey. Frequently lions react to the sounds of animals walking or moving through water and set out to investigate and see for themselves what is causing the disturbance. This faculty is, of course, particularly valuable at night. On the other hand, the sense of smell appears to be underutilized in alerting the lion to the nearness of quarry. It is quite normal for a large group of potential victims to pass by during the night and not be noticed by sleeping lions. In general, lions hunt only what they can see.

Two lionesses slowly stalk a group of antelope known as topi, using their keen eyesight to observe the movements of the animals and to determine which of them will be the easiest to take.

summer, when the land is parched by heat and glaring light, herds of zebras and gazelles flock to rivers and lakes for relief. This activity stirs lions to a flurry of surreptitious stalking and pouncing that is frequently rewarded.

Senses

More than any of the senses, sight is all important to lions as hunters. Like all cats, they have excellent vision, both in full daylight and in

Here the overwhelming might of a lion's body can be seen, as it uses the strength of its legs and the power of its shoulders and hindquarters to press a victim to the ground and kill it quickly.

A lioness sits quietly in the grass, looking out onto the plain. She is perfectly still and seems peaceful enough, but her keen eyesight and good hearing are at work as she tracks the movements of prey.

A zebra has been brought down by two adult females, and they look to their cubs, waiting close by, to join them for the meal. They will share the food according to rank within the pride, and the division of the meal may lead to squabbles and fights among the group's members.

Four cubs eagerly share a meal. The intestines and organs are the most nutritious parts of any animal and are easier than muscle for young lions to bite off and digest.

Hunting Strategies

The lion appears not to be as proficient a hunter as other predators. Its almost complete dependence on sight causes it to frequently betray its cover. Furthermore, it pays little attention to the wind's direction, allowing its scent to be carried ahead to warn prey animals of danger.

Yet, prey is so abundant in the lion's habitat that these shortcomings matter little. In their domains in East and Central Africa, lions are greatly outnumbered by the herbivores they hunt. Generally, they kill about one in fifteen of the zebras, gazelles, and other animals in the area. It is estimated that the number of animals taken by lions through much of Africa roughly equals the number lost during the annual drought. In short, though they alone have only a slight effect on the large populations of these creatures, the predation of lions, when combined with death by natural causes and the activities of other predators, helps to control the numbers of herd animals and maintain a natural balance.

Lions are able to overcome their inefficiencies as hunters through cooperation. Sometimes an entire pride will join in an attack. In such a case, several lions slowly circle a herd and edge the animals toward other lions hiding in tall grasses. At the right moment, the concealed lions leap at the prey from the sides or from behind, usually concentrating on one of the slower, weaker animals.

Group hunting also compensates for the lion's lack of prolonged swiftness. Although they are not slow—their maximum speed is 30 miles (48 kilometers) per hour—stamina is a problem. They rarely chase an animal for more than 100 yards (91 meters). However, by working in groups, surrounding an animal and attacking from several directions, they are able to capture prey that might otherwise be too

Once the victim has been chosen, and as soon as it is close enough, the lion charges forward in a sudden burst of speed to make the kill. The weak and unwary are easily taken, but alert, swift creatures have a chance of escape.

With almost military precision and a thorough understanding of the role each will play, a group of lions arranges itself into a line of attack. The intended victim will be taken through cooperation and concerted effort.

Lions prefer to eat all freshly killed food at one time. Depending on the size of their meal, they may not need to hunt again for three to four days.

This hapless topi is typical of the grazing herd animals that form the greater part of the lion's diet. The weight of the average kill is around 250 pounds (112.5 kilograms), which is sufficient to feed six to eight lions.

Though lions are capable of hunting alone, they often cooperate with other pride members to take on larger, stronger prey. Here, two female lions work in tandem to bring down a Cape buffalo.

Lions and hyenas are vicious rivals. Hyenas not only prey on lion cubs, but large packs of them occasionally drive small prides away from their own kills. Here, a lone hyena pays the price for harassing a male lion.

quick or elusive for them as solitary hunters.

Once the kill is made, the group settles down to share the meal. No part of the carcass is wasted, for lions are inclined to consume all of their fresh food immediately. Only if the prey is too large to be eaten right away will lions remain in the vicinity to guard the carcass against scavengers and other predators. They may even try to hide it in a concealed place until they are hungry again.

When lions start to feed, they usually begin with the victim's intestines, which is the most nutritious part of the meal. After that, they consume the meat, working forward from the hindquarters. The average kill weighs about 250 pounds (112.5 kilograms), from which a pride of six lions can obtain a meal of about 40 pounds (18 kilograms) each.

Following a substantial meal, lions rest for at least twenty-four hours. Since they tend to consume all the food they have, sometimes eating as much as 75 pounds (34 kilograms) each at one time, rest periods can be quite long. Prides have been observed gorging themselves for several hours and then moving very little for as many as four days. By the fifth day, they began to walk around, and by the sixth, they were again ready to hunt.

Aside from the number of lions in this pride, the sheer size of the dominant females illustrates the value of cooperative hunting. There can be few large animals that could withstand a determined attack, launched from all directions, made by these powerful cats.

Male lions living in prides take little part in hunting, leaving this job to the able females. However, once an animal has been taken, the male comes forward to feed first and to take the "lion's share" of the choicest portions.

LION WATCHING

The lion, a wide-ranging animal in past millennia, is today found only in certain parts of Africa, a continent it once entirely dominated. Despite its survival there in relatively healthy numbers, the African lion has not been without threat.

The spread of human populations and agricultural and industrial development in this century have had their effects on the environment and wildlife. The list of vanished wilderness areas and extinct or endangered animals is a long one and still growing. The continent of Africa has faced this problem as much as any other. The usual elements—human encroachment, alteration or destruction of habitat, excessive hunting, and poaching—have wiped once thriving species off the map in numerous regions of Africa.

At one time, not many years ago, the world faced a future in which its was feared that such magnificent creatures as the elephant and the lion would soon no longer exist in the wild.

Luckily, this trend has been halted, if not entirely reversed, by a combination of factors, from the growing strength of the conservation and ecology movements to the African peoples' awareness of the value of wildlife as a tourist attraction. In the past thirty years, the countries of Africa have made great efforts to preserve and protect their wildlife populations.

Today, there are dozens of nationally sponsored game parks and reserves where the animal life thrives almost as it did before the arrival of European ideas of progress. Still, it is worth noting that no matter how large some of these areas may be, they are only a fraction of the land these animals once roamed freely. For instance, Kenya's vast system of national parks adds up to just over 7 percent of the nation's total land area.

Animal lovers benefit from the national park systems, not only in knowing that the lion's survival is ensured, but in having the opportunity to observe these animals in action. Tourist facilities and guided tours are now widely available and offer thousands of people a once-in-a-lifetime opportunity to study wildlife at close range. Some of the best parks for watching lions are described in the following pages.

Female lions drink from a pool on the floor of the Ngorongoro Crater in Tanzania. They are members of one of the six prides that live there, completely cut off from the outside world by the high walls of the extinct volcano.

A well–camouflaged young cub settles into the protective grasses of Kenya's Masai Mara Game Reserve.

Kenya's Tsavo National Park contains many different kinds of land-scapes in which lions can be seen. The big cats are peaceful today, but a hundred years ago, at the height of colonial expansion, many in this area were known as man-eaters.

Masai Mara is typical lion country with its broad stretches of sweeping, grassy plains, dotted with scrub trees and low underbrush. Here, a stately lioness watches a rainstorm as it moves across the landscape, bringing welcome relief from the heat of the day.

KENYA

Kenya, of all the African nations, has the greatest number of parks and tourist facilities, with reserves offering many chances for seeing and studying lions.

Masai Mara Game Reserve

The Masai Mara is made up of the Kenyan portion of the Serengeti Plain, which it shares with Tanzania, and is, therefore, part of one of the largest wilderness and wildlife reserves in the world. Many sizable lion prides are found here.

The lions find abundant prey due to the yearly migration of millions of herd animals traveling through Tanzania to the south. The huge, open spaces of the reserve, covering 720 square miles (1,872 square kilometers), provide splendid views of the lion population.

Nairobi National Park

Located just outside the Kenyan capital, Nairobi, the park is a twenty-minute drive

from a bustling city to a spot where lion prides, zebras, wildebeests, and cheetahs are found. The juxtaposition of modern civilization and the wilderness is dramatic. With the city's skyline visible from various points in the park, it is possible to watch a lion stalk its prey while a jumbo jet crosses the horizon in the background.

Samburu National Reserve
The reserve is in the dry, northern part of the country. Its rugged, arid landscape supports little covering vegetation, thereby offering clear views of the lion population. At the park's lodges, it is often possible to see lions come very near to obtain bait.

Tsavo National Park
Tsavo has been so configured that it forms eastern and western sectors. Encompassing 9,000 square miles (23,400 square kilometers), this park is a huge rambling area containing a variety of habitats, ranging from marshlands to mountainous regions. Here, lions can be seen, amidst a wide diversity of creatures, living in a setting that recalls the wild state of Africa in the past.

Meru National Park
This park has a special place in the hearts of lion lovers because of its association with zoologists Joy and George Adamson and the lioness Elsa, heroine of the best-selling book, *Born Free,* and the popular film of the same name. Lying along the equator to the west of Mount Kenya and bisected by thirteen rivers and numerous mountain-fed streams, Meru contains 320 square miles (832 square kilometers) of diverse habitats such as mountain woodlands, broad plains, and wandering riverbanks. The mountainous western section is lush and green, while the eastern sector is semiarid. This area is very remote and difficult to reach. It is, therefore, almost completely unspoiled.

A female lion suns herself on one of the riverbanks of the Samburu National Reserve in Kenya. Lions are wary of water and avoid full immersion in it. In this, they are unlike tigers who are enthusiastic and skilled swimmers.

TANZANIA

Tanzania contains some of the most legendary wildlife reserves anywhere, from Serengeti and the fascinating Ngorongoro Crater, to Mount Kilamanjaro. In this region, lions roam over the sites of the earliest known human fossil remains.

Lake Manyara National Park

Set along the Great Rift, Lake Manyara is a beautiful area of dramatic landscapes with 130 square miles (338 square kilometers) of parkland. Actually, most of the total area is taken up by the lake itself which is home to a million or so pink flamingos.

Here, lions prove false the once widely held belief that they do not climb. In fact, the Lake Manyara lions are often seen resting in tree branches, whiling away the time until nightfall. The area is relatively unspoiled by human encroachment due to the prevalence of the tsetse fly.

Ngorongoro Crater

Although it makes up only a small portion of the conservation area, the Ngorongoro Crater is the main attraction here. The remains of an extinct volcano, its 100-square-mile (260-square-kilometer) floor is home to six separate lion prides. Naturalists have named each pride after different aspects of the crater.

The Ngorongoro Crater is in effect an island, cut off from the surrounding area. This isolation has had its good and bad aspects. The crater has one of the densest wildlife populations in Africa, making the lions' search for prey quite easy. However, the islandlike setting has kept out the migration from other areas of lions with fresh genetic strains, leading to dangerous inbreeding. Over one hundred lions inhabit the crater, while over three thousand live outside.

Serengeti National Park

The Serengeti National Park contains the greatest number of large African animals anywhere on the continent. The park stretches across nearly 6,000 square miles (15,600 square kilometers) of hills and plains. Vast herds of wildebeests, buffalo, gazelles, zebras, and others are spread across the area. The lion population enjoys such an abundance of prey

As a lioness shrewdly takes in the activity on the Serengeti Plain at twilight, some of the many grazing animals that inhabit the area can be seen in the background.

Ngorongoro lions, because of their isolation, are endangered by the increasing problem of inbreeding. Another major problem in recent years has been the outbreak of tormenting, bloodsucking flies.

that the prides seldom need to go outside their ranges. Serengeti is operated with a minimum of tourist facilities and attractions, thus making it the most unspoiled of all the great national parks in East Africa.

SOUTH AFRICA

Though lions have not fared well in this country due to development, there are still a few noteworthy lion-watching sites. Kruger National Park is South Africa's largest game reserve and the last home of the Transvaal lion, a subspecies that was indigenous to the southeast tip of the continent. In the smaller Kalahari Gemsbok National Park, the stark landscape offers many unobstructed views of the big cats in their daily pursuits.

The lions of the Lake Manyara area of Tanzania are known for tree climbing and tree sitting. Some spend entire days perched high in a comfortable branch.

A pride shares a meal at Kalahari Gemsbok National Park in South Africa. Lions are largely nocturnal hunters, and feed mostly during the hours between dusk and dawn.

Queen Elizabeth National Park in Uganda is home to yet another group of tree-climbing lions. Threatened by violence and civil war in the past, the park today takes great care to nurture its massive wildlife population.

UGANDA

Queen Elizabeth National Park is Uganda's largest game reserve. Set against the Ruwenzori Mountains, it is a rich and beautiful region with a varied topography. For lion watchers, the place to go is the southern section of the park, called Ishasha. Difficult to reach at times, Ishasha is considered one of the best preserved game-viewing areas in Africa.

What distinguishes the lions in this 30-square-mile (78-square-kilometer) park is their propensity for climbing into the local fig trees and resting in their branches. It is not uncommon to come across two or three lions sleeping in a bough—a startling sight and one seen regularly only in Tanzania's Lake Manyara reserve. It is not certain why the lions of Queen Elizabeth indulge in this habit. Some believe it is to escape the biting flies, which can be a major nuisance on the ground.

INDIA

Far removed from their African cousins, the lions of Gir National Park and Lion Sanctuary are the only remaining colony of Indian, or Asiatic, lions. Even this enclave came very close to being wiped out, and continues to have a questionable future due to human encroachments, such as the herds of grazing domesticated cattle that force out the lions' natural prey.

The Gir lion population now numbers 250 animals, but visitors will find them far from elusive. Gir lions have learned to live with the presence of humans and their vehicles, making close observation almost certain. The park, closed during the monsoon season, is at its best for lion watching between December and May.

THE LION'S FUTURE

The lion is here to stay, at least for the foreseeable future. Unlike so many other animals in this century, African lions are not among those listed on any endangered species list, and none of the major remaining lion populations of Africa face any immediate threat of extinction.

However, there is still much to be done. Illegal hunting and poaching have to be continuously monitored, and conservation policies must not be allowed to erode by allowing commercial interests to intrude in any way upon presently established wilderness areas. Furthermore, research within these areas should be ongoing to ensure continued genetic diversity and prevent inbreeding.

Through the centuries, humans have done much to honor the lion's existence and much to threaten it. It is hoped that future interactions between people and lions will emphasize the honor and put an end to the threat.

No matter where he is seen— whether in Kenya, Tanzania, South Africa, or India— the noble lion, either in action or in repose, is the monarch of the animal kingdom.

71

INDEX

*Page numbers in **bold-face** type indicate photo captions.*